Project 369
Manifestation Journal

Manifest Your Dreams

"If you only knew the magnificence of the 3, 6 and 9, then you would have the key to the universe."

Nikola Tesla

The energy we put out into the world is the energy we get back from it, this is the basic idea of the law of attraction. According to the law, your thoughts and inner desires affect your reality, you get what you think about, whether you want it or not.

Our desires manifest into our world by the energy we dedicate to them.

There are plenty of techniques used to manifest our dreams, one of these techniques is the 369, popularized by the great Serbian scientist Nikola Tesla.

How to use this journal:

◉ Every morning, shortly after you're awake. Write down your affirmation three times.

◉ Midday. You will write down your affirmation six times.

◉ In the evening, before going to sleep. Write your affirmation nine times while thinking about what you want to manifest.

Repeat these steps for 33 to 45 days while taking action and working towards your goals and they will surely manifest.

Keep in mind when using this journal, you should always:

◉ Clearly state what you want to manifest.

◉ Be in a good and happy mental state when writing your desires.

◉ Try to be patient. The universe work mysteriously.

◉ Keep a close eye on the signs in your life. They are incredibly important.

It's also important that you don't force a particular timeline. Also, keep in mind that the universe works in mysterious ways, your dreams will surely manifest but they will manifest at the right time in your life.

what will you be manifesting?

Date: ___ / ___ / ___

Morning Affirmation

1. _____

2. _____

3. _____

Afternoon Intention

1. _____

2. _____

3. _____

4. _____

5. _____

6. _____

369 Method

Evening Goal / Desired Action

1.
2.
3.
4.
5.
6.
7.
8.
9.

Date: ___ / ___ / ___

Morning Affirmation

1.

2.

3.

Afternoon Intention

1.

2.

3.

4.

5.

6.

369 Method

Evening Goal / Desired Action

1.

2.

3.

4.

5.

6.

7.

8.

9.

Date: ___ / ___ / ___

Morning Affirmation

1.

2.

3.

Afternoon Intention

1.

2.

3.

4.

5.

6.

369 Method

Evening Goal / Desired Action

1.

2.

3.

4.

5.

6.

7.

8.

9.

Date: ___ / ___ / ___

Morning Affirmation

1.

2.

3.

Afternoon Intention

1.

2.

3.

4.

5.

6.

369 Method

Evening Goal / Desired Action

1.

2.

3.

4.

5.

6.

7.

8.

9.

Date: ____ / ____ / ____

Morning Affirmation

1.

2.

3.

Afternoon Intention

1.

2.

3.

4.

5.

6.

369 Method

Evening Goal / Desired Action

1.

2.

3.

4.

5.

6.

7.

8.

9.

Date: ___ / ___ / ___

Morning Affirmation

1.

2.

3.

Afternoon Intention

1.

2.

3.

4.

5.

6.

369 Method

Evening Goal / Desired Action

1.

2.

3.

4.

5.

6.

7.

8.

9.

Date: ___ / ___ / ___

Morning Affirmation

1.

2.

3.

Afternoon Intention

1.

2.

3.

4.

5.

6.

369 Method

Evening Goal / Desired Action

1.
2.
3.
4.
5.
6.
7.
8.
9.

Date: ___ / ___ / ___

Morning Affirmation

1.

2.

3.

Afternoon Intention

1.

2.

3.

4.

5.

6.

369 Method

Evening Goal / Desired Action

1.

2.

3.

4.

5.

6.

7.

8.

9.

Date: ___ / ___ / ___

Morning Affirmation

1.

2.

3.

Afternoon Intention

1.

2.

3.

4.

5.

6.

369 Method

Evening Goal / Desired Action

1.

2.

3.

4.

5.

6.

7.

8.

9.

Date: ___ / ___ / ___

Morning Affirmation

1.

2.

3.

Afternoon Intention

1.

2.

3.

4.

5.

6.

369 Method

Evening Goal / Desired Action

1.
2.
3.
4.
5.
6.
7.
8.
9.

Date: ___ / ___ / ___

Morning Affirmation

1. _____

2. _____

3. _____

Afternoon Intention

1. _____

2. _____

3. _____

4. _____

5. _____

6. _____

369 Method

Evening Goal / Desired Action

1.
2.
3.
4.
5.
6.
7.
8.
9.

Date: ___ / ___ / ___

Morning Affirmation

1.

2.

3.

Afternoon Intention

1.

2.

3.

4.

5.

6.

369 Method

Evening Goal / Desired Action

1.

2.

3.

4.

5.

6.

7.

8.

9.

Date: ___ / ___ / ___

Morning Affirmation

1.
2.
3.

Afternoon Intention

1.
2.
3.
4.
5.
6.

369 Method

Evening Goal / Desired Action

1.

2.

3.

4.

5.

6.

7.

8.

9.

Date: ___ / ___ / ___

Morning Affirmation

1. _____

2. _____

3. _____

Afternoon Intention

1. _____

2. _____

3. _____

4. _____

5. _____

6. _____

369 Method

Evening Goal / Desired Action

1.

2.

3.

4.

5.

6.

7.

8.

9.

Date: ___ / ___ / ___

Morning Affirmation

1.

2.

3.

Afternoon Intention

1.

2.

3.

4.

5.

6.

369 Method

Evening Goal / Desired Action

1.

2.

3.

4.

5.

6.

7.

8.

9.

Date: ___ / ___ / ___

Morning Affirmation

1.

2.

3.

Afternoon Intention

1.

2.

3.

4.

5.

6.

369 Method

Evening Goal / Desired Action

1.

2.

3.

4.

5.

6.

7.

8.

9.

Date: ___ / ___ / ___

Morning Affirmation

1.

2.

3.

Afternoon Intention

1.

2.

3.

4.

5.

6.

369 Method

Evening Goal / Desired Action

1.

2.

3.

4.

5.

6.

7.

8.

9.

Date: ___ / ___ / ___

Morning Affirmation

1.

2.

3.

Afternoon Intention

1.

2.

3.

4.

5.

6.

369 Method

Evening Goal / Desired Action

1.

2.

3.

4.

5.

6.

7.

8.

9.

Date: ___ / ___ / ___

Morning Affirmation

1.

2.

3.

Afternoon Intention

1.

2.

3.

4.

5.

6.

369 Method

Evening Goal / Desired Action

1.

2.

3.

4.

5.

6.

7.

8.

9.

Date: ___ / ___ / ___

Morning Affirmation

1.

2.

3.

Afternoon Intention

1.

2.

3.

4.

5.

6.

369 Method

Evening Goal / Desired Action

1.
2.
3.
4.
5.
6.
7.
8.
9.

Date: ___ / ___ / ___

Morning Affirmation

1.

2.

3.

Afternoon Intention

1.

2.

3.

4.

5.

6.

369 Method

Evening Goal / Desired Action

1.

2.

3.

4.

5.

6.

7.

8.

9.

Date: ___ / ___ / ___

Morning Affirmation

1.

2.

3.

Afternoon Intention

1.

2.

3.

4.

5.

6.

369 Method

Evening Goal / Desired Action

1.

2.

3.

4.

5.

6.

7.

8.

9.

Date: ___ / ___ / ___

Morning Affirmation

1.

2.

3.

Afternoon Intention

1.

2.

3.

4.

5.

6.

369 Method

Evening Goal / Desired Action

1.

2.

3.

4.

5.

6.

7.

8.

9.

Date: ___ / ___ / ___

Morning Affirmation

1.
2.
3.

Afternoon Intention

1.
2.
3.
4.
5.
6.

369 Method

Evening Goal / Desired Action

1.

2.

3.

4.

5.

6.

7.

8.

9.

Date: ___ / ___ / ___

Morning Affirmation

1.

2.

3.

Afternoon Intention

1.

2.

3.

4.

5.

6.

369 Method

Evening Goal / Desired Action

1.

2.

3.

4.

5.

6.

7.

8.

9.

Date: ___ / ___ / ___

Morning Affirmation

1.

2.

3.

Afternoon Intention

1.

2.

3.

4.

5.

6.

369 Method

Evening Goal / Desired Action

1.

2.

3.

4.

5.

6.

7.

8.

9.

Date: ___ / ___ / ___

Morning Affirmation

1. _____

2. _____

3. _____

Afternoon Intention

1. _____

2. _____

3. _____

4. _____

5. _____

6. _____

369 Method

Evening Goal / Desired Action

1.

2.

3.

4.

5.

6.

7.

8.

9.

Date: ___ / ___ / ___

Morning Affirmation

1.

2.

3.

Afternoon Intention

1.

2.

3.

4.

5.

6.

369 Method

Evening Goal / Desired Action

1.

2.

3.

4.

5.

6.

7.

8.

9.

Date: ___ / ___ / ___

Morning Affirmation

1. _____

2. _____

3. _____

Afternoon Intention

1. _____

2. _____

3. _____

4. _____

5. _____

6. _____

369 Method

Evening Goal / Desired Action

1.
2.
3.
4.
5.
6.
7.
8.
9.

Date: ___ / ___ / ___

Morning Affirmation

1. _____

2. _____

3. _____

Afternoon Intention

1. _____

2. _____

3. _____

4. _____

5. _____

6. _____

369 Method

Evening Goal / Desired Action

1.

2.

3.

4.

5.

6.

7.

8.

9.

Date: ___ / ___ / ___

Morning Affirmation

1. _____

2. _____

3. _____

Afternoon Intention

1. _____

2. _____

3. _____

4. _____

5. _____

6. _____

369 Method

Evening Goal / Desired Action

1.

2.

3.

4.

5.

6.

7.

8.

9.

Date: ___ / ___ / ___

Morning Affirmation

1.

2.

3.

Afternoon Intention

1.

2.

3.

4.

5.

6.

369 Method

Evening Goal / Desired Action

1.
2.
3.
4.
5.
6.
7.
8.
9.

Date: ___ / ___ / ___

Morning Affirmation

1. _____

2. _____

3. _____

Afternoon Intention

1. _____

2. _____

3. _____

4. _____

5. _____

6. _____

369 Method

Evening Goal / Desired Action

1.

2.

3.

4.

5.

6.

7.

8.

9.

Date: ___ / ___ / ___

Morning Affirmation

1.
2.
3.

Afternoon Intention

1.
2.
3.
4.
5.
6.

369 Method

Evening Goal / Desired Action

1.

2.

3.

4.

5.

6.

7.

8.

9.

Date: ____ / ____ / ____

Morning Affirmation

1.

2.

3.

Afternoon Intention

1.

2.

3.

4.

5.

6.

369 Method

Evening Goal / Desired Action

1.

2.

3.

4.

5.

6.

7.

8.

9.

Date: ___ / ___ / ___

Morning Affirmation

1. _____

2. _____

3. _____

Afternoon Intention

1. _____

2. _____

3. _____

4. _____

5. _____

6. _____

369 Method

Evening Goal / Desired Action

1.

2.

3.

4.

5.

6.

7.

8.

9.

Date: ___ / ___ / ___

Morning Affirmation

1.
2.
3.

Afternoon Intention

1.
2.
3.
4.
5.
6.

369 Method

Evening Goal / Desired Action

1.

2.

3.

4.

5.

6.

7.

8.

9.

Date: ___ / ___ / ___

Morning Affirmation

1.

2.

3.

Afternoon Intention

1.

2.

3.

4.

5.

6.

369 Method

Evening Goal / Desired Action

1.
2.
3.
4.
5.
6.
7.
8.
9.

Date: ___ / ___ / ___

Morning Affirmation

1.
2.
3.

Afternoon Intention

1.
2.
3.
4.
5.
6.

369 Method

Evening Goal / Desired Action

1.

2.

3.

4.

5.

6.

7.

8.

9.

Date: ___ / ___ / ___

Morning Affirmation

1.
2.
3.

Afternoon Intention

1.
2.
3.
4.
5.
6.

369 Method

Evening Goal / Desired Action

1.
2.
3.
4.
5.
6.
7.
8.
9.

Date: ____ / ____ / ____

Morning Affirmation

1.

2.

3.

Afternoon Intention

1.

2.

3.

4.

5.

6.

369 Method

Evening Goal / Desired Action

1.

2.

3.

4.

5.

6.

7.

8.

9.

Date: ___ / ___ / ___

Morning Affirmation

1.

2.

3.

Afternoon Intention

1.

2.

3.

4.

5.

6.

369 Method

Evening Goal / Desired Action

1.

2.

3.

4.

5.

6.

7.

8.

9.

Date: ___ / ___ / ___

Morning Affirmation

1.
2.
3.

Afternoon Intention

1.
2.
3.
4.
5.
6.

369 Method

Evening Goal / Desired Action

1.

2.

3.

4.

5.

6.

7.

8.

9.

Date: ___ / ___ / ___

Morning Affirmation

1.

2.

3.

Afternoon Intention

1.

2.

3.

4.

5.

6.

369 Method

Evening Goal / Desired Action

1.

2.

3.

4.

5.

6.

7.

8.

9.

Date: ___ / ___ / ___

Morning Affirmation

1.
2.
3.

Afternoon Intention

1.
2.
3.
4.
5.
6.

369 Method

Evening Goal / Desired Action

1.

2.

3.

4.

5.

6.

7.

8.

9.

Date: ___ / ___ / ___

Morning Affirmation

1.

2.

3.

Afternoon Intention

1.

2.

3.

4.

5.

6.

369 Method

Evening Goal / Desired Action

1.
2.
3.
4.
5.
6.
7.
8.
9.

Date: ___ / ___ / ___

Morning Affirmation

1.

2.

3.

Afternoon Intention

1.

2.

3.

4.

5.

6.

369 Method

Evening Goal / Desired Action

1.

2.

3.

4.

5.

6.

7.

8.

9.

Date: ____ / ____ / ____

Morning Affirmation

1. _____

2. _____

3. _____

Afternoon Intention

1. _____

2. _____

3. _____

4. _____

5. _____

6. _____

369 Method

Evening Goal / Desired Action

1.
2.
3.
4.
5.
6.
7.
8.
9.

Date: ___ / ___ / ___

Morning Affirmation

1. _____

2. _____

3. _____

Afternoon Intention

1. _____

2. _____

3. _____

4. _____

5. _____

6. _____

369 Method

Evening Goal / Desired Action

1.

2.

3.

4.

5.

6.

7.

8.

9.

Date: ___ / ___ / ___

Morning Affirmation

1.

2.

3.

Afternoon Intention

1.

2.

3.

4.

5.

6.

369 Method

Evening Goal / Desired Action

1.

2.

3.

4.

5.

6.

7.

8.

9.

Date: ___ / ___ / ___

Morning Affirmation

1.

2.

3.

Afternoon Intention

1.

2.

3.

4.

5.

6.

369 Method

Evening Goal / Desired Action

1.
2.
3.
4.
5.
6.
7.
8.
9.

Date: ___ / ___ / ___

Morning Affirmation

1.

2.

3.

Afternoon Intention

1.

2.

3.

4.

5.

6.

369 Method

Evening Goal / Desired Action

1.
2.
3.
4.
5.
6.
7.
8.
9.

Date: ___ / ___ / ___

Morning Affirmation

1. ___
2. ___
3. ___

Afternoon Intention

1. ___
2. ___
3. ___
4. ___
5. ___
6. ___

369 Method

Evening Goal / Desired Action

1.

2.

3.

4.

5.

6.

7.

8.

9.

Date: ___ / ___ / ___

Morning Affirmation

1.

2.

3.

Afternoon Intention

1.

2.

3.

4.

5.

6.

369 Method

Evening Goal / Desired Action

1.
2.
3.
4.
5.
6.
7.
8.
9.

Date: ___ / ___ / ___

Morning Affirmation

1.

2.

3.

Afternoon Intention

1.

2.

3.

4.

5.

6.

369 Method

Evening Goal / Desired Action

1.
2.
3.
4.
5.
6.
7.
8.
9.

Date: ___ / ___ / ___

Morning Affirmation

1.

2.

3.

Afternoon Intention

1.

2.

3.

4.

5.

6.

369 Method

Evening Goal / Desired Action

1.

2.

3.

4.

5.

6.

7.

8.

9.

Date: ___ / ___ / ___

Morning Affirmation

1. _____

2. _____

3. _____

Afternoon Intention

1. _____

2. _____

3. _____

4. _____

5. _____

6. _____

369 Method

Evening Goal / Desired Action

1.

2.

3.

4.

5.

6.

7.

8.

9.

Date: ___ / ___ / ___

Morning Affirmation

1.

2.

3.

Afternoon Intention

1.

2.

3.

4.

5.

6.

369 Method

Evening Goal / Desired Action

1.

2.

3.

4.

5.

6.

7.

8.

9.

Your feedback is what keeps us going.
Please feel free to leave
an honest review on our amazon page.

Printed in Great Britain
by Amazon